THE ROOFTOPS OF PARIS

THE ROOFTOPS OF PARIS

Photography
NICOLAI CANETTI

Commentary
SANDY LESBERG

A HADDINGTON HOUSE BOOK
Distributed by THE BOBBS-MERRILL CO. INC.

FIRST PUBLISHED 1976 BY
PEEBLES PRESS INTERNATIONAL
12 Thayer St., London W1M 5LD
10 Columbus Circle, New York, N.Y. 10019

DESIGNED BY NICOLAI CANETTI

© Peebles Press International (Europe) Ltd
ISBN 0–672–52219–5
Library of Congress Catalog No. 75–36330

Distributed by
The Bobbs-Merrill Co. Inc.
4300 West 62nd St., Indianapolis, Indiana 46268, U.S.A
in the United States and Canada

WHS Distributors
Euston St., Freemens Common, Leicester, England
in the U.K., Ireland, Australia, New Zealand and South Africa

Meulenhoff-Bruna B.V.
Beulinstract 2, Amsterdam, Netherlands
in the Netherlands

Printed and bound in the U.K.
Redwood Burn Limited, Trowbridge and Esher

Paris is a great romantic notion, a city where manner and style are far more important than sum and substance, and where the emphasis is generally placed on how one feels rather than what one does. It is a splendid conspiracy of sensory perceptions that rely not a whit on such traditional municipal supports as people or commerce or art or literature. Here there is a unique sense of place, a glorious impress of touch and smell and above all, feel, that cannot be found anywhere else. Try to reproduce in your mind's eye any other city where you have been a visitor. You may remember the details sharp and clear but how much can you feel of the city in your memory? Do you recall the colours of the awnings on the shops, the odours of the bakeries and delicatessens, can you place yourself in the rhythm of the people striding along the sidewalks?

And now remember Paris.

All other cities are the same as some other cities, but no one can ever mistake Paris for anything but herself.

Here you walk for an hour, two hours, sit in a cafe, sip an apperitif, wander through a museum, float in and around a street market, talk to no one and be talked to by no one. Yet there is no feeling of isolation. You have rather become a part of the city vital. Your investment is small, you are merely there, but your reward is startling. This a warm, soft atmosphere that will accommodate all of us without discrimination. It is seductive by inattention. The buildings have soft lines, the colours are warm, the shops attractive and even the simplest food is almost unreproachable. There is neither an imperial nor a proleterian visage to be found here as in other, more unsubtle, European capitals untutored in the art of gentle communication. The face of Paris is a lush invitation to be pleasured beyond all reasonable surface expectations. And if, during the process, you should be stirred deeply or moved passionately you will in some indefinable way be assuming a certain innocence that allows a rebirth of interest in all the exhilerating things of life.

Some are less kind about the city. A mere walk along the Champs Elysees, they imply, is not necessarily vitalizing. A brush with the student-riddled St. Michel is not so amusing. There is no joy in merely viewing the Opera House nor in strolling along the Seine harassing the bookstall owners. Pretty is, is NOT as pretty does. The surface has been scratched and the lustre has dimmed. Paris is a lady, they shrug, who has been notoriously generous with her charms for too long and her good graces have now begun to fray at the edges. She has answered too many calls to duty from seekers of the truth through too many ages, all clutching her benefices too ardently. And now her beauty has frailed and her charm is gaunt and wan. These sceptics admit that Paris was once uniquely and richly attractive but claim that her *joi de vivre* has been self-defeating. These Philistines, Parisians all, fear for the survival of her spirit.

Never mind, for I know them well, and I suspect they are merely trying to keep her for themselves. It is not her way, exclusivity. She is for all of us.

It is sheer delight to look out across the rooftops of Paris, and to contemplate the city beneath them. They are distinctive, delicious (more so the ugly ones), unpredictable in their association one with the other, and can never be confused with the rooftops of any other city on earth. They are the first layer of the Parisian sweet cake, the gay *châpeau*, the crown that signals your attention below. They are the funny irresistable magnets that draw us to the sheer magic of the streets.

They are the signposts of Paris.

This is the St. Michel area on the Left Bank.
It looks like the perfect place to hole up and write a novel.

Two views of the fantastic Champs Elysées looking down from the Arc de Triomphe. Below you can see the famous restaurant Fouquet's on the right, at the corner of the Avenue George V.

Note the three sky pointers, all different.

This is from the Arc de Triomphe.

The city is full of lively red punctuations.

Here's a French lad perched at the top of the Arc de Triomphe, looking at a long view of Montparnasse in the distance accented by the Eiffel Tower.

A flower vendor near the Palais Royal and the Comedie Française.
This is where Colette and Jean Cocteau used to live (separately).
Not far from here, across the street, the cafe where Napoleon used to play chess is still operating.

One of the more pleasant benefits of Parisian life -- strolling near the Boulevard St. Germain de Prés.

A bustling street scene — Rue Montmartre — the Folies Bergère is just around the corner.

A small study involving the Seine, a solitary figure, some classic Parisian apartment buildings and in the misty background, a modern highrise.

Luxembourg Gardens.

Night scenes. At the top, the Hotel de Ville de Paris. Below, a government administration building on the other side of the Seine.

Some slashing views from the Gare d'Est.

The headquarters of the influential newspaper Figaro.

The old Les Halles district.

Here are some views from the roof of the Hotel Napoleon considered by many to be the finest first-class hotel of its size in all of Paris — located a few giant steps from the Arc de Triomphe, it is full of Napoleonic memorabilia (an invoice for the Emperor's boots for instance), and boasts an intimate bar and one of the best Alsatian restaurants anywhere. It is a perfect example of the marriage of style and convenience.

The modern is sadly almost overwhelming the traditional.

The Hotel Depart bids farewell to an old friend.

Pizza, dragons and sex : a Parisian bouillabaisse.

OVERLEAF Montmartre.

Pigalle.

A nice sunny look at the Towers of Sacré Coeur.

The Eiffel Tower seen from Montmartre.

Paris rooftops all mixed up with television antennae.

Pigeons on the grass, not alas, on the way up the hill to Sacré Coeur.

Let's watch a few solitary Parisians watching us from their windows.

Did you spot the watchers? This is the drugstore in St. Germain de Prés, and there is one person up there watching us.

He'll be right back!

Can you see the painting on the wall inside the window?

Not all the artists in Paris are on the sidewalk . . .

... Not all the balconies are used for painting.

A pair of converted gaslamps.

Television antennae challenging the Eiffel Tow

The simple act of feeding birds at the base of the hill,
emphasises the majesty of Sacré Coeur.

A graphic illustration of how *la belle époque*
coexists with *l'époque moderne.*

View from the Eiffel Tower looking over the Trocadero.

Yes, this is George Washington, seated to no one's surprise in the Place Washington.

WASHINGTON

The Arc de Triomphe tucked away in the midst of a busy modern city.

One of the most distinguished streets in Paris – l'Avenue de l'Opera.

A fantastic view of Paris from the Seine all the way up the hill to the Sacré Coeur, on Montmartre.

Paris seen from the top of Nôtre Dame.

OVERLEAF   The gargoyles of Nôtre Dame keeping watch
over the city of Paris.

The square in front of Nôtre Dame.

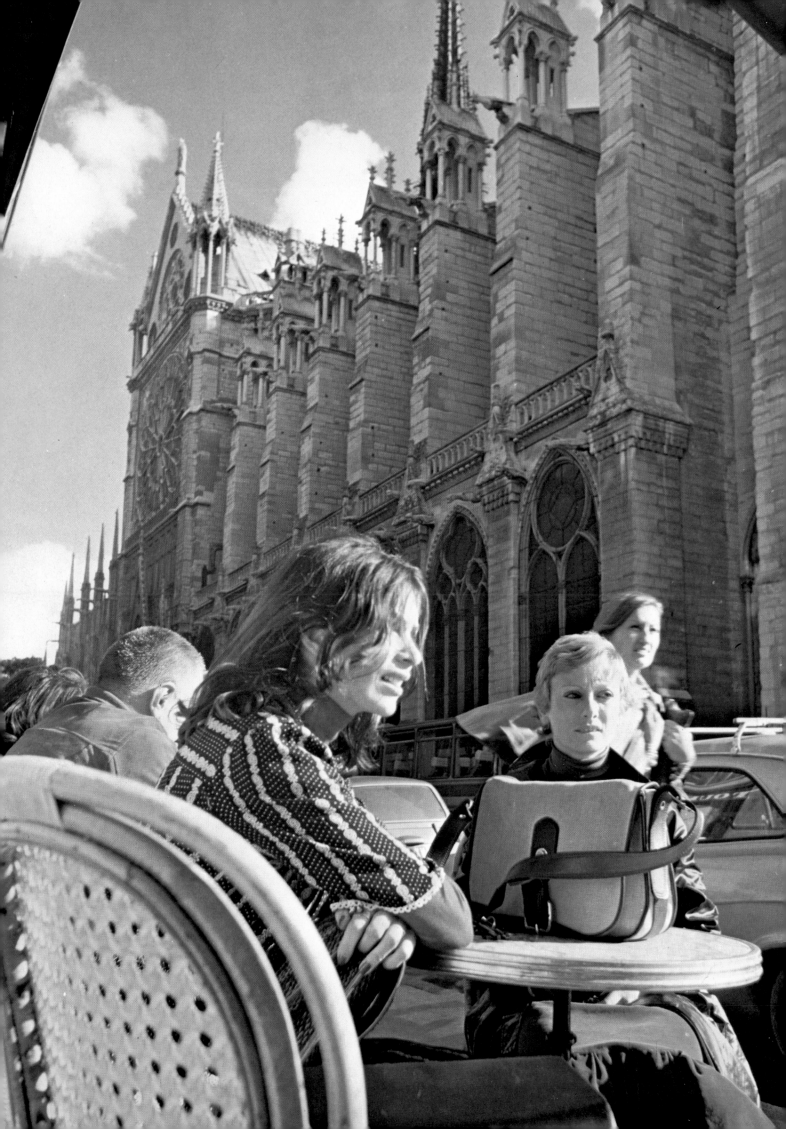